Klapholz

by Patricia White • COOKIES!

PIE!

77 wonderful recipes for Pies savory & sweet:
SAVORY: the best of Quiches, Oyster Pie
& Green Tomato Pie, Chicken Pie, Pork Pie
& English Steak & Kidney Pie
SWEET: old-fashioned Apple Pie, Custard & Pumpkin Pies,
Meringues & Berry Pies & New England Cobblers —
Plus all the secrets of baking Pie

by Patricia White

DECORATIONS BY MEL KLAPHOLZ

SIMON AND SCHUSTER • NEW YORK

First Printing

SBN 671-20367-3
Library of Congress Catalog Card Number: 71-84134
Designed by Eve Metz
Manufactured in the United States of America

1506873

To Sylvie

CONTENTS

Introduction

To a great many people a homemade pie is something glowingly remembered from childhood as the coveted finale to a festive meal, seldom seen from one holiday to the next. What a pity it is that people today think pie baking is difficult. Homemade pies are worth every minute of time and elbow grease expended in their preparation, and one good homemade pie will make all others inadequate; even bakery-shop pies won't match up.

So bolster up your courage and bake one completely from scratch. No ready-made pie shell, no prepared filling. It should be enough to make that childhood memory a reality. And it will be nice to find in this day of ready-made everything that some of the good things of yesterday are still among the good things of today.

BASIC EQUIPMENT

Given the right equipment, baking is not a chore, and creating a pie can be marvelous fun. For the basic equipment to make the job a great deal easier, I would suggest:

MIXING BOWLS Have several sizes to accommodate both filling and dough, one large enough to allow you to mix the dough easily. A large, shallow bowl is best for this as it allows you to blend ingredients quickly and keeps over-mixing to a minimum.

MEASURING CUPS AND SPOONS Have at least two measuring cups, one for liquids and one for dry ingredients. A set of graduated measuring spoons is also useful.

PASTRY BLENDER This is a wonderful invention which makes the cutting in of shortening easy. This can also be accomplished with two knives, but not as well.

ELECTRIC MIXER This is an essential for making meringue and angel pies. It is also good for preparing hot water pastry. You can live without one, but if you have only a rotary beater, creating chiffon and cream pies won't be as much fun as it should be. A portable mixer is probably more useful than a big table model.

PASTRY CLOTH AND SLEEVE FOR ROLLING PIN Pastry cloths are made of heavy linenlike canvas, and they simplify rolling out pastry. The idea is to run a fair quantity of flour into the cloth, thereby impregnating it so the dough won't stick to it. Dough is then rolled out on the cloth and lifts off without sticking (just try rolling out dough on a Formica counter top and you'll see why you need a pastry cloth). If your pastry cloth slips, put a lightly dampened dish towel underneath before rolling out dough. A sleeve for your rolling pin acts as a pastry cloth does — it keeps the dough from sticking to the pin. Pastry cloths and sleeves are usually sold together.

10

The heavier the rolling pin, the better, but in addition to being heavy your pin must move easily. I find a small-to-medium-size more useful than an enormous pin, because I have limited work space. But if you have the room, a big pin will get the job done faster.

PIE PANS   Pie pans come in many sizes and shapes, and even casserole dishes may be considered pie pans for deep-dish pies and cobblers. Measure top inside diameter for size. Most recipes call for 9-inch pie pans, though 8- and 10-inch pans are also commonly used. Be sure that the pan is made of a nonshiny material (shiny pans reflect the heat and pies made in them don't brown evenly). I prefer glass to dull aluminum, but that is a personal preference.

COOLING RACK   I used to think it was unnecessary for pie baking until I finally bought one — and now it has become an essential in my kitchen. The important feature of a cooling rack is that it gets the pie pan off a flat surface and allows air to circulate under it. This enables the pie to cool evenly and lessens the chance of soggy bottom crusts. A cooling rack can be one particularly designed for the purpose or it can be any rack you can find that allows a free flow of air. My own was designed as an outdoor grill and is a rectangular box with two layers of grillwork.

PIE SERVER   A proper wedge-shaped pie server eliminates making a hash out of pies while serving as it gives the slice something to rest upon as it is transferred to the plate.

PASTRY MAKING

Basically there are two methods of making pastry — with ice water or with hot water. Each has its own adherents, who have their own reasons for liking the method they choose. Both turn out flaky, even pastry.

General rules are the same for making both types of pastry. However made, pastry should be flaky, delicate and tender, and when broken should show layers of flat flakes with air spaces between. This flakiness is achieved by the quick, deft handling of dough which causes the shortening to break up into minute particles, each surrounded by flour which absorbs the shortening during baking and forms a flat flake. Over handling of dough — the usual cause of tough, unevenly browned pastry — causes the shortening and flour to become totally combined and solid.

Your dough is mixed when it forms a ball in the mixing bowl and comes away clean from the sides of the bowl. Then divide the dough into two parts (assuming you are making a two-crust pie). Lightly flour the pastry cloth and rolling pin and its sleeve, if using one. Do not over-flour, as excess flour clinging to the dough can make the dough hard. Roll the dough quickly, lightly and evenly in one direction with each stroke. Start in the center of the dough ball and roll to the edge. Try to keep the dough as circular as possible, for this saves patching the crust once the dough is turned into the pie pan. The dough should be consistent in thickness, to assure even baking and browning. As you roll, keep pin free of maverick pieces of dough that may cling. Dough should be about $1/8$ inch thick and rolled large enough to fill pie pan amply —

that is, enough to line the pan, cover the rim and make an attractive ridge. I find the easiest way to line the pie pan with a minimum of tearing of the dough is to place the pan face down in the middle of the rolled-out dough and then, with one hand gently holding the pie pan in place, reverse the pastry cloth, thereby turning the dough into the pan without peeling it off the pastry cloth first. Then gently peel off pastry cloth and lightly tap dough into pan, making sure that no air is trapped between pan and pastry. If you are going to bake the pastry shell unfilled, be certain to prick bottom crust to remove any airpockets (it is a good idea to prick every crust as a rule of thumb) and pour in some uncooked dry navy beans or rice to weight it down while baking, so it can't tent up. (The beans can be kept in a jar and used over and over.)

Trim the bottom crust to allow for an ample rim. If there is to be no top crust, flute or pinch rim now (either with your fingers or with the tines of a fork). This rim should be even in depth to assure even browning, and wide enough to cover rim of pie pan.

Roll out top crust in the same way — it can be a bit narrower. When filling has been distributed evenly over bottom crust, reverse pastry cloth with the top crust centered over the pie and peel off. Adjust top crust if necessary, and trim. With fingers or tines of a fork, pinch rim of top and bottom crusts together. Slash top crust in several places to allow steam to escape. Glaze (see page 21) as desired. For decorative lattice or partial top crusts, see page 19.

PASTRY RECIPES

The flour in these recipes should be plain, not self-rising, flour.

HOT WATER PASTRY

¾ cup plus 2 tablespoons solid vegetable shortening *at room temperature* (or butter or margarine; not lard)

¼ cup boiling water
1 teaspoon salt
1 tablespoon milk
2¼ cups flour, sifted

Combine shortening, boiling water, salt and milk in a mixing bowl and with an electric mixer beat at medium speed until smooth and fluffy. With a spatula, blend in flour until dough clings together and cleans the bowl. Again, do not overmix.

ICE WATER PASTRY

2 cups flour, sifted
1 teaspoon salt
¾ cup solid vegetable shortening, or butter or margarine. For lard see page 15
¼ cup ice water (you may need a bit more)

Blend flour, salt together in a mixing bowl and cut in shortening with a pastry blender until dough has the consistency of coarse cornmeal. Add ice water a tablespoonful at a time and toss with fork until dough clings together. Do not overmix — blend only until dough clings together. Too much water will produce sticky dough that makes a soggy pie crust.

14

PASTRY MADE WITH LARD (especially good for meat pies)

2 cups flour, sifted
1 teaspoon salt

½ cup lard, cold
3 tablespoons cold water

Sift flour and salt together and cut in lard with a pastry blender until dough looks like coarse cornmeal. Sprinkle with water, a tablespoonful at a time and mix together until blended. Shape dough into a ball with hands, gently and quickly.

PASTRY MADE WITH OIL (easiest recipe to measure and blend)

2 cups flour, sifted
1 teaspoon salt

½ cup vegetable oil (not olive, butter flavored, or peanut)
3 tablespoons ice water

Sift flour and salt together. Add oil and toss with a fork. Sprinkle with water, a tablespoonful at a time, and blend quickly. Gently shape dough into a ball with hands — do not knead.

CHEESE PASTRY (wonderful for fruit pies, quiches or vegetable pies)

2¹/₂ cups flour, sifted
¹/₂ teaspoon salt
1¹/₂ cups grated sharp American cheese

²/₃ cup solid shortening
¹/₃ cup ice water

Sift flour and salt together. Cut in American cheese and shortening with a pastry blender until mixture has the texture of coarse cornmeal. Sprinkle with ice water, a tablespoonful at a time, and blend until dough holds together.

COOKIE DOUGH FOR OPEN-FACED FRUIT PIES
(very rich and slightly chewy)

2¹/₂ cups flour
1 teaspoon baking powder
¹/₂ cup sugar

2 tablespoons butter
1 egg, beaten
¹/₂ cup milk

Sift dry ingredients together and cut in butter. Add egg and milk and blend together until mixed. Roll out about ¹/₄ inch thick, flute edges and fill with any recipe for fruit pie. (Makes two 9-inch bottom crusts.)

CRUMB CRUSTS (Baked and Unbaked)

Crumb crusts are crisper and hold their shape better when baked and cooled before filling, but unbaked crumb crusts take less time to make. If you are using an unbaked crumb crust, be sure to refrigerate it before filling. Making crumbs from whole cookies is easily done in a blender, or by rolling between sheets of foil.

BAKED CRUMB CRUST FOR ONE 9-INCH PIE
Graham Cracker: 1⅓ cups crumbs (18 crackers), ¼ cup sugar, ¼ cup butter
Gingersnap: 1⅓ cups crumbs (20 cookies), ¼ cup sugar, ⅓ cup butter
Chocolate: 1⅓ cups crumbs (18 cookies), ⅓ cup sugar, ¼ cup butter
Vanilla: 1⅓ cups crumbs (20 cookies), ⅓ cup sugar, ¼ cup butter
Zwieback: 1⅓ cups crumbs (12 biscuits), ⅓ cup sugar, ¼ cup butter

VARIATIONS
Marble: Add two grated squares unsweetened chocolate to 1 cup crumbs, ⅓ cup sugar and ¼ cup butter
Nut: Add ½ cup chopped nuts to 1 cup crumbs, ⅓ cup sugar and ¼ cup butter.
Spice: Add 1 teaspoon cinnamon and ½ teaspoon ginger to vanilla recipe

Blend all ingredients together (be sure butter is soft) and pat into pie pan with the back of a tablespoon. With your thumb as a pusher, form an even rim around the outside edge of pie plate. Be sure the edge is even or it will not bake uniformly or it will crack and break off. Bake for 10 minutes at 350°. Cool before filling.

UNBAKED CRUMB CRUSTS FOR ONE 9-INCH PIE
Graham Cracker: 1⅓ cups crumbs (18 crackers), ¼ cup brown sugar, 1 teaspoon cinnamon, ⅓ cup melted butter
Pretzel: 1 cup crumbs (14 round pretzels), ¼ cup sugar, ¼ cup soft butter

Cookie Crumb: 1⅓ cups crumbs, ¼ cup sugar, ¼ cup soft butter
Peanut Butter: 2 cups graham cracker crumbs (26 crackers), ¼ cup sugar, ¼ cup crunchy peanut butter, 1 tablespoon water

Mix all ingredients thoroughly and line pie pan as with baked crumb crusts. Refrigerate several hours before filling.

MISCELLANEOUS CRUSTS

NUT CRUSTS
Mix 1 cup ground nuts (pecans or walnuts are best) with 2 tablespoons sugar. Line pie plate with mixture, but do not spread on rim. Refrigerate before filling.

TOASTED COCONUT CRUST
Mix together 2 tablespoons soft butter with 1½ cups shredded coconut. Line pie pan with mixture and bake for about 20 minutes at 325°, until crust is browned. Cool before filling.

MERINGUE PIE CRUST

4 egg whites
¼ teaspoon salt

1 teaspoon lemon juice
1 cup sugar

Beat egg whites at highest speed until foamy. Add salt and lemon juice and continue beating. Gradually add sugar, a tablespoon at a time, and beat until stiff and glossy. Spread in a greased 9-inch pie pan and bake in a 275° oven for about 1¼ hours. If you have a generous filling for the meringue, be sure to mound the unbaked meringue up well in the pie pan. When baked, cool pan on a cooling rack until meringue can be slipped out of pie pan. Fill and serve cold.

DECORATIVE TOP CRUSTS AND EDGINGS

Even the most basic of pies can be dressed up to look handsome.

I think that most fruit and berry pies look best with a lattice or twisted lattice top crust. A well-woven lattice crust is impressive and easy to make. Prepare a basic pastry dough, divide in half, roll out bottom crust, line pie pan, prick and fill with filling of your choice. Roll out the remaining dough as you did for the bottom crust. It should be about 1/8 to 1/4 inch thick (better to be thin than thick). With a pizza cutter or pastry cutter (one with a jagged edge is prettiest), cut uniform strips of dough about 1/4 to 1/2 inch wide. Cut as many strips as you can to fit across your pie pan with enough overlap to seal the ends of the strips to the edge of the bottom pie crust. Reserve trimmed ends and short strips to roll out again if necessary to finish the top crust. Weave the crust (either wide apart or closely as you wish) by laying one strip across the middle of the pie, turning the pan and laying the next strip at right angles to the first strip, and so on until your crust is woven. Trim the overhang of the lattice strips and press trimmed ends into the edges of the bottom crust. Flute the edges evenly, or gently press together with the tines of a fork.

For a twisted lattice top crust, roll out dough as above and cut with a pastry cutter. When the strips are cut, gently turn the ends of each strip to form a spiral and proceed to weave as above. Or cut the dough about $1/2$ to 1 inch wide and lay the spirals in one direction only. Making a twisted lattice top takes a bit of practice and deft handling, particularly if you're making a big pie. If the result is not quite as gorgeous as you had intended, take heart and try again.

A variation on the lattice top is to lay strips of dough straight across the center of the pie, at two-inch intervals all around the edge — each strip will bisect the pie, giving the effect of marking the top crust for cutting.

A full top crust can be dressed up by making decorative slits (needed anyway to let the steam escape). Decorative slits are easier to make neatly before putting the top crust on the unbaked pie. So, after the top crust is rolled out, and while it is still on the pastry cloth, use a sharp knife to make stars, diamonds or whatever small shape you fancy. Gently remove dough from within the marked shapes before putting the crust on the pie. Very small cookie cutters are also useful for this. With a little practice, you will also be able to use the excess bits of dough to garnish the outside of the pie. They can be cut into little circles or leaves or other shapes, or even into someone's initials for a special occasion.

Simply moisten the underside of the shape with a little beaten egg and gently press it to the top crust. Glaze as desired and bake.

EDGES

Pretty edges improve the appearance of any pie. The standard fluted edge is made by folding the overhang of an untrimmed pie shell (one or two crusts) under and turning the pastry up to make a rim that stands up. Put the index finger of your right hand on the inside of the pastry rim to secure it, and with the thumb and index finger of your left hand pinch pastry to form rounded fluting. Space flutings every ½ inch.

Another pretty edging is made by again folding overhang under and turning up. With the tines of a fork (dipped in cold water) gently press down dough evenly around.

GLAZES FOR TOP CRUSTS

Glazes make top crusts shiny, the pies brown better and have a more decorative appearance. Sugar (the coarser granulated kind is best) sprinkled over an uncooked glaze gives a pie crust a sparkled surface when baked. Almost any liquid shortening — melted butter, margarine, vegetable oil — can be used, as can milk, cream, ice water or evaporated milk. But for the shiniest, smoothest surface, a well-beaten whole egg or egg white is champion.

DISASTER AREAS

PASTRY PROBLEMS
Tough Pastry is usually the result of incorrect measuring or overhandling. Be sure that the ratio of flour, shortening and liquid is exactly as called for. The beginning pie baker seldom underhandles pastry dough and often overhandles it. Pastry ingredients must be completely blended but

never kneaded together. The less you handle dough once it has begun to come clean off the sides of the mixing bowl, the better. Rolling and rerolling over and over again has the same effect as kneading, so try to have to roll out each crust only once.

Crumbly Pastry is the result of too much shortening and too little water, or dough that hasn't been mixed enough. It can also be the result of pastry rolled too thin. The edges of the pie shell should not break off when gently touched.

Shrunken Pie Shell comes either from stretching the pie dough when lining the pie pan, or from rolling unevenly. If you have to patch a pie shell, do it carefully, so that you don't create a lumpy patch on an even surface. Shrunken cookie-crumb crusts result from uneven distribution over pie pan. Crumb crusts require a little extra care in pressing them down evenly.

Tents are caused by insufficient pricking or weighting down of bottom crusts. See page 13 to avoid this.

Uneven Browning is not always the baker's fault. If your oven heat is uneven, your baking will be uneven. Ovens can be adjusted and should be if the difference in heat from front to back is very noticeable. You can turn a pie halfway around in mid baking, so it is back to front, and finish baking. But this is really not recommended, as the baking time has to be adjusted to allow for opening the oven door. And for pies that rise (like quiche), it causes more harm than good. But if the fault is not with your oven, you may want to check that you haven't under-baked your pie, or used shiny baking pans (or placed the pie pan on a shiny aluminum baking sheet) which deflect heat away. Faulty dough can also be to blame, generally caused by too much liquid and too little shortening, or the overhandling of dough.

Uneven browning is also caused by a pie placed too high or too low in the oven. Always bake in the middle of the center rack away from the oven walls. An edge fluted very high, or insufficient filling to hold a top pie crust can also cause uneven browning.

Soggy Crust is usually caused by under baking or by faulty dough. Be careful when pricking bottom crust not to make holes through which the filling can seep. Once you have assembled a pie, particularly a fruit pie, be sure to bake it right away. Do not let it stand unbaked for any length of time, or the pastry dough will start to absorb the juices and become soggy even before it's baked.

Filling that Spills Over can come from using too much filling or not enough thickening. If the fruit you're using is very ripe and juicy, you may have to add a bit more cornstarch, tapioca or flour to the recipe. Be sure to cut sufficient air vents in a two-crust pie to let the steam escape or you are sure to have massive spill-over. These vents should be toward the center of the pie, not near the edge. Also be sure the top and bottom crusts are well sealed together to eliminate the filling leaking out the side. A funnel inserted in the middle of a fruit pie will let the extra juices bubble up in it and eliminate messy spill-over.

be long on cornstarch filling and short on fruit. And the flavor and texture of canned pie filling doesn't approach that of fresh.

Frozen, unbaked fruit pies and frozen, ready-to-defrost-and-serve cream, custard and chiffon pies have been greatly improved since they first came on the market. Fruit pies as a whole tend to be skimpy on filling, but this varies greatly between brands, and you should try a number to see which you like best. Most apple and peach pies seem to be somewhat pallid in flavor, and you might remove the top crust with a sharp knife before baking, and give them a sprinkling of cinnamon, nutmeg and grated lemon peel. To reseal top crust, simply dampen the underside of the edge of the top crust with water or beaten egg and pinch edges of top and bottom crusts together. If you're going to jazz up a frozen pie, be sure to do so when it is completely hard frozen to lessen the chance of cracking the top crust.

Savory Pies

QUICHES
SEAFOOD PIES
VEGETABLE PIES
MEAT PIES

QUICHES

The word "Quiche" has become a classification for main dish or hors d'oeuvres custard pies, usually flavored with vegetables, meat or seafood. These pies have a single pastry crust and are filled with delicate custard. Quiches do not keep well for the most part and should be eaten the day they are made. Reheating a quiche is generally a disaster and destroys the fluffy texture that makes them a delight. Any leftover quiche should be kept at room temperature and eaten as soon as possible.

For variety, try making quiches with cheese pastry crusts.

QUICHE LORRAINE

Type of pie: main dish or hors
d'oeuvres
Baking time: 45 minutes
Preheat oven to: 375°
Pie pan: 10-inch pie pan
Type of crust: pastry, single crust
Quantity: serves six as an entrée, ten
to twelve as hors d'oeuvres

½ recipe for two-crust pastry (see
pages 14 and 15)
8 slices bacon, cooked crisp and
crumbled
6 eggs, beaten until smooth
1 large yellow onion, minced
2½ cups half and half (or half milk,
half cream)
2 tablespoons melted butter

1 tablespoon Worcestershire sauce
1½ teaspoons salt
½ teaspoon nutmeg
1 pound Swiss cheese, grated coarsely
⅛ teaspoon cayenne pepper
¼ teaspoon coarsely ground black
pepper
¼ cup Parmesan cheese, grated

*The original French/Swiss Cheese-and-Onion pie, from which all other
quiche variations derive. Serve hot, warm or at room temperature, for
lunch or light supper; or cut in bite-size pieces for hors d'oeuvres.*

Prepare pastry as directed on pages 14 and 15, line pie pan and flute
edges. Scatter bacon over bottom of pastry. In a bowl, mix together beaten
eggs, minced onion, half and half, melted butter, Worcestershire sauce,
salt, nutmeg, Swiss cheese, cayenne pepper and black pepper. Pour mixture into pie shell. Sprinkle top with grated Parmesan and bake for 15

29

minutes in 375° oven. Reduce temperature to 325° and bake another 30 minutes. Serve immediately as an entrée, or cool on a cooling rack and serve at room temperature for hors d'oeuvres.

SEAFOOD QUICHE

Type of pie: main dish
Baking time: 35 minutes
Preheat oven to: 375°
Pie pan: 9-inch baking pan
Type of crust: Pastry, single crust
Quantity: serves four as an entrée, six to eight as hors d'oeuvres

---

1/2 recipe for two-crust pastry
3 tablespoons chopped onion
2 tablespoons butter
6 1/2-ounce can flaked crabmeat (rinsed once and thoroughly drained)
8-ounce can minced clams (rinsed once and thoroughly drained)
1/3 cup sherry

1 teaspoon monosodium glutamate (MSG)
3 eggs
2/3 cup sour cream
1/2 teaspoon salt
1/8 teaspoon pepper
1/8 teaspoon nutmeg
1/8 teaspoon thyme
1/2 cup shredded Swiss cheese

This is a marvelous entrée, light but substantial. It lends itself to the addition of cooked shrimp or lobster meat for company serving.

Prepare pastry and line pie pan. Flute edges. In a small frying pan, sauté onion in butter until transparent but not browned. Add drained crabmeat and clams, sherry and MSG and heat through. Remove from heat. In a medium bowl, beat together eggs, sour cream, salt, pepper, nutmeg and thyme. Fold in seafood mixture and stir to blend. Pour into pie shell and sprinkle top with shredded Swiss cheese. Place on lower rack of oven and bake at 375° for about 35 minutes. The top should be browned. Cool for 10 minutes before slicing as an entrée. Or cool to room temperature if serving as hors d'oeuvres.

CHIVE QUICHE

Type of pie: main dish or hors d'oeuvres
Baking time: 55 minutes
Preheat oven to: 450°
Pie pan: 9-inch pie pan
Type of crust: pastry, single crust
Quantity: serves four as an entrée, six to eight as hors d'oeuvres

---

½ recipe for two-crust pastry
1½ cups chive cottage cheese (or 1½ cups creamed cottage cheese and ¼ cup snipped chives)
½ cup shredded Swiss cheese

4 eggs
⅓ cup half and half
⅛ teaspoon white pepper
1½ teaspoon salt
¾ cup canned French fried onion rings (one can)

This pretty quiche makes an unusual entrée for lunch or a light supper.

Prepare pastry, line and flute edges. Bake at 450° for 10 minutes. Cool.

Lower oven temperature to 350°. Beat together cottage cheese, Swiss cheese, eggs, half and half, pepper and salt until smooth. Fill cooled pie shell and bake for 35 minutes. Top with onion rings and bake another 10 minutes. Cool on a cooling rack.

MUSHROOM QUICHE

Type of pie: main dish
Baking time: 25 minutes
Preheat oven to: 450°
Pie pan: 9-inch pie pan
Type of crust: pastry, single crust
Quantity: serves four to six

1/2 recipe for two-crust pastry	4 eggs
3/4 pound fresh, whole mushrooms	2 cups half and half
4 tablespoons butter	1/2 teaspoon nutmeg
2 medium yellow onions, finely chopped	1/2 teaspoon MSG
	1/2 teaspoon coarsely ground pepper

Prepare pastry, line pan and flute edges. Chop mushrooms fine and sauté until wilted in 2 tablespoons butter. Reduce heat to low and cover pan, simmering mushrooms for about 20 minutes. Bake pastry for about five minutes and cool until ready for filling. Sauté onion in 2 tablespoons butter until soft but not brown. Blend until smooth all other ingredients, fold in mushrooms and onions. Pour into partially baked pie shell. Bake 15 minutes at 450°, lower temperature to 350° and bake about another 10 minutes until puffy and lightly browned. Serve hot.

TOMATO QUICHE

Type of pie: main dish
Baking time: 55 minutes
Preheat oven to: 450°
Pie pan: 10-inch pie pan
Type of crust: pastry, single crust
Quantity: six servings

½ recipe for two-crust pie
5 eggs
1½ cups half and half
1 teaspoon MSG
1 teaspoon mixed salad herbs
¼ teaspoon coarsely ground pepper

¼ cup minced scallions
3 tablespoons minced parsley
3 medium, firm ripe tomatoes, halved
    with cores removed
½ teaspoon basil
¼ teaspoon seasoned salt
1 teaspoon sugar

This attractive quiche has halves of tomatoes set in quiche custard.

Prepare pastry, line pan, flute edges. Bake at 450° for five minutes. Remove from oven and lower oven temperature to 350°. In a bowl combine eggs, half and half, MSG, salad herbs, ground pepper, scallions and parsley until thoroughly blended. Pour into partially baked pie shell. Place tomato halves around edge of pie, then sprinkle with mixed basil, seasoned salt and sugar. Bake about 50 minutes. Cool on a cooling rack.

SAUSAGE QUICHE

Type of pie: main dish or hors
  d'oeuvres
Baking time: 45 minutes
Preheat oven to: 375°
Pie pan: 9-inch pie pan
Type of crust: pastry, single crust
Quantity: serves four as an entrée, six
  to eight as hors d'oeuvres

1/2 recipe for two-crust pastry
1 pound pork sausage meat
1 medium onion, finely chopped
1/2 pound Swiss cheese, grated
1 tablespoon flour
4 eggs

1 1/2 cups half and half
1/2 teaspoon seasoned salt
1/4 teaspoon coarsely ground pepper
1/2 teaspoon nutmeg
2 tablespoons chopped parsley
1 teaspoon sage

A wonderful dish to serve for Sunday brunches or light suppers.

Prepare pastry, line pan and flute edges.

 Fry sausage meat until crisp and brown. Lumps of sausage should be no bigger than peas. Drain sausage meat and remove from pan. Sauté chopped onion in sausage fat until transparent, remove from fat and put with sausage. Line pie pan with 3/4 of sausage and all the onion. Sprinkle cheese over sausage and onion and dust 1 tablespoon flour over cheese. Beat together eggs, half and half, salt, pepper, nutmeg, parsley, and sage until thoroughly blended. Pour over meat, onion and cheese and scatter remaining sausage on top. Bake for about 45 minutes (look at pie after 40 minutes) until quiche is set. Cool on a cooling rack before cutting.

1506873

SHRIMP PIE

Type of pie: main dish
Baking time: 15 to 20 minutes
Preheat oven to: 450°
Pie pan: 8-inch pie pan
Type of crust: pastry, lattice top
Quantity: four to six servings

---

1 recipe for two-crust pastry
1 pound cleaned, shelled shrimp (frozen or fresh)
1 cup water
½ cup chopped onion
3 tablespoons butter
1½ cups fresh tomatoes, peeled and chopped

½ cup fresh mushrooms, sliced
1 teaspoon seasoned salt
¼ teaspoon coarsely ground black pepper
4 tablespoons flour
1 hard-boiled egg, chopped
12 black olives, pitted and sliced
1 egg, beaten, for brushing

Simmer shrimp in water, covered, for five minutes. Remove from pan, drain reserving ¾ cup of liquid, and chop coarsely. Sauté chopped shrimp and onions in butter until tender. Add tomatoes, mushrooms, shrimp stock, salt, pepper and flour. Simmer, covered, for 15 minutes.

Prepare pastry, roll out and line pie pan with half of it. Fill with shrimp mixture and sprinkle with chopped egg and olives. Weave a lattice crust and flute edges together. Brush with beaten egg and bake about 15 minutes in 450° oven until crust is browned and filling is bubbly.

SALMON PIE

Type of pie: main dish
Baking time: 35 minutes
Preheat oven to: 350°
Pie pan: 9-inch pie pan
Type of crust: pastry, single crust
Quantity: four to six servings

½ recipe for two-crust pastry
3 eggs, beaten
1½ cups canned or cooked salmon,
    boned and flaked

1½ cups milk
2 tablespoons chopped chives
1 tablespoon chili sauce
1 teaspoon MSG

A delicate, light pie for luncheons or light suppers.

Prepare pastry and line 9-inch pie pan, fluting edges high. Combine all other ingredients and blend well. Pour into pastry-lined pie pan and bake about 35 minutes until filling is set and the crust is browned. Garnish with parsley before serving.

FISH PIE

Type of pie: main dish
Baking time: 50-55 minutes
Preheat oven to: 400°
Pie pan: 9-inch pie pan
Type of crust: pastry, single crust
Quantity: six main dish servings

$^1/_2$ recipe for two-crust pastry
2 pounds fresh or frozen fish fillets
(ocean perch, sole, flounder)
$^1/_4$ cup butter, melted
2 teaspoons seasoned salt
$^1/_2$ teaspoon pepper
2 tablespoons flour

1 cup liquid from cooking fish (add
milk to make up 1 cup)
$^1/_4$ cup cracker crumbs
$^1/_2$ cup chopped mushrooms (fresh,
preferably)
3 hard-boiled eggs, quartered
2 large, ripe tomatoes, sliced
3 tablespoons coarsely chopped parsley

Place fish on a rack in a baking pan, brush with 2 tablespoons of the melted butter, then place in the oven and bake at 400° for 15 minutes. Fish should be firm, but should flake easily with a fork. Remove from accumulated juices and set aside. Measure juices and add milk if necessary to make 1 cup.

In a saucepan combine remaining melted butter with seasoned salt, pepper and flour, blending until smooth. Add fish juices and milk.

Combine cracker crumbs with mushrooms and layer pie pan with mushroom mixture, quartered eggs, tomato slices, parsley and flaked fish so that there are two layers of each ingredient. Pour butter and fish-juice sauce over all.

Prepare and roll out pastry. Cover pie and flute edges. Slash to let steam escape, and bake for about 35 minutes until pastry is well browned.

OYSTER AND SWEETBREAD PIE

Type of pie: main dish
Baking time: 30 minutes
Preheat oven to: 400°
Pie pan: deep-dish casserole, 6-cup size
Type of crust: pastry, single crust
Quantity: six main dish servings

1/2 recipe for two-crust pastry
2 pair sweetbreads
1 tablespoon vinegar
3 tablespoons butter
3 tablespoons flour
1 cup half and half
1 cup chicken broth

1/2 teaspoon seasoned salt
1/4 teaspoon coarsely ground pepper
1 teaspoon Worcestershire sauce
1/2 teaspoon celery seed
1 tablespoon finely chopped parsley
1 pint oysters with their liquor
a little milk, for brushing

An unusual pie with a marvelous subtle flavor.

Soak sweetbreads in cold water for 15 minutes. Transfer to a saucepan filled with salted water to which you add 1 tablespoon vinegar. Parboil for 20 minutes; remove from boiling water and plunge immediately into cold water. When cold, cut away membranes and slice into 1/2-inch cubes.

In a frying pan, melt butter and dust in flour, stirring constantly. Slowly add half and half and broth, stirring until smooth and thickened. Add all other ingredients (except pastry) and heat through. Pour into casserole. Roll out pastry and top casserole, making sure to extend pastry well over the edges. Slash well. Brush crust with milk and bake casserole about 30 minutes until crust is browned and the filling bubbly.

GREEN TOMATO PIE

Baking time: 30 minutes
Preheat oven to: 425°
Pie pan: 9-inch pie pan
Type of crust: pastry, single crust
Quantity: six servings

1/2 recipe for two-crust pastry
2 1/2 cups green tomatoes, thinly sliced
1/4 cup dark brown sugar
1 teaspoon cinnamon
1/2 teaspoon nutmeg

1/2 teaspoon allspice
1/2 teaspoon mustard
2 tablespoons light corn syrup
2 tablespoons lemon juice
2 tablespoons water
3 tablespoons flour

The goodness of green tomatoes is legend to country people, and this is one of the best recipes for them.

Prepare pastry, roll out and line pie pan. Flute edges. Mix together, gently, all other ingredients and turn into unbaked pie shell. Bake about 30 minutes, until pastry is browned and tomatoes are tender.

EGGPLANT PIE

Baking time: 45-50 minutes
Preheat oven to: 375°
Pie pan: 9-inch pie pan
Type of crust: pastry, single crust
Quantity: six vegetable or ten hors d'oeuvre servings
Storing: in refrigerator, covered

½ recipe for two-crust pastry
2 cups eggplant, cubed and unpeeled
¼ cup butter
1 cup fresh mushrooms, coarsely chopped
½ cup scallions, chopped
1 clove garlic, minced

2 tablespoons parsley, coarsely chopped
½ cup celery tops, chopped
½ teaspoon seasoned salt
½ teaspoon MSG
1 teaspoon mixed salad herbs
¼ cup tomato paste

This pretty pie of many colors can be served hot or chilled, or cut in thin slices as hors d'oeuvres.

Prepare pastry, roll out and line 9-inch pie pan. Flute edges. Sauté eggplant in butter, covered, for ten minutes over low heat. Add all other fresh ingredients and cook until mushrooms begin to wilt, stirring constantly. Add salt, MSG, herbs and tomato paste. Stir once to mix and turn into pie shell. Bake for about 45-50 minutes until filling is bubbly and crust is browned. Cool slightly before serving.

CREAMED SPINACH PIE

Baking time: 45 minutes
Preheat oven to: 375°
Pie pan: 9-inch pie pan
Type of crust: pastry, single crust
(try cheese pastry for variety)
Quantity: six to eight servings
Storing: in refrigerator, covered

½ recipe for two-crust pastry
¼ lb. sliced bacon
1 cup chopped onion
one 10-ounce package frozen chopped
    spinach

1 cup milk
4 eggs, beaten
1 teaspoon seasoned salt
½ teaspoon MSG
½ teaspoon nutmeg

Prepare pastry, roll out and line pie pan. Flute edges.

Fry bacon until crisp. Drain and crumble. Sauté onion in bacon fat until golden. Cook spinach as package directs. Drain well. Puree spinach (a blender does this easiest) with milk. Add beaten eggs, salt, MSG and nutmeg to spinach puree. Line uncooked pastry with bacon and onions and pour spinach mixture over them. Bake pie for about 45 minutes until filling is set. Cool slightly before serving.

BRUSSELS SPROUT PIE

Baking time: 45 minutes
Preheat oven to: 325°
Pie pan: 9-inch pie pan
Type of crust: pastry, single crust
   (try cheese pastry for variety)
Quantity: serves six
Storing: in refrigerator, covered

$^1/_2$ recipe for two-crust pastry
one 10-ounce package frozen baby
   Brussels sprouts
$^1/_2$ pound thinly sliced bacon, cooked,
   drained and crumbled
2 cups Swiss cheese, grated

2 eggs, beaten
$^1/_2$ teaspoon salt
$^1/_2$ teaspoon MSG
$^1/_4$ teaspoon coarsely grated black
   pepper
1 cup heavy cream
1 tablespoon chopped chives

*This is an excellent choice when you are serving a light entrée and want
a substantial vegetable to accompany it.*

Prepare pastry, line pan and flute edges. Thaw Brussels sprouts, drain
and chop coarsely. Combine sprouts, bacon and cheese and spread over
unbaked pie shell. Combine all other ingredients and pour over sprout
mixture. Bake for about 45 minutes (mixture should be firm), slice and
serve immediately.

CHICKEN PIE

Baking time: approximately 1 hour
(filling ½ hour, crust ½ hour)
Preheat oven to: 375°
Pie pan: deep-dish casserole, 1½ quart
Type of crust: pastry, single crust
Quantity: four to six servings
Storing: in refrigerator, covered

½ recipe for two-crust pastry
1 young 3-pound roasting chicken
water
6 tablespoons flour
2 tablespoons butter
½ teaspoon seasoned salt
1 teaspoon MSG
2 hard-boiled eggs, quartered
½ teaspoon pepper, coarsely
    ground

FORCEMEAT NO. 1
¼ pound dry old bread
2 teaspoons chopped parsley
½ teaspoon thyme
finely grated rind ½ lemon

Forcemeat, No. 1, *continued*
½ teaspoon seasoned salt
⅛ teaspoon paprika
⅛ teaspoon cayenne
½ stick butter (4 tablespoons), softened
1 egg yolk
½ stick butter for browning forcemeat
    balls
1 egg yolk, beaten, for brushing

FORCEMEAT NO. 2
liver and heart of chicken
¼ pound sausage meat
1 teaspoon chopped parsley
1 teaspoon chopped chives
½ teaspoon seasoned salt

This old English recipe is well worth the time it takes to prepare.

Bone chicken and cut the meat into bite-size pieces. Cover bones, wings, and neck with water, and simmer to make stock. Dredge chicken pieces

43

in flour and sauté in butter until browned lightly; dust with seasoned salt and MSG, cover and continue cooking for about 20 minutes. Turn as needed.

Make forcemeats by blending ingredients together with fingers and forming balls about the size of small walnuts. Brown forcemeat balls in 4 tablespoons butter until lightly browned.

Line casserole with combined chicken, quarters of hard-boiled eggs and forcemeat balls. Combine the drippings from pans in which chicken and forcemeat have been browned with 1/2 cup of the stock made from the chicken bones, and pour over casserole.

Prepare, roll out and cover casserole with pastry crust. Brush rim of casserole with beaten egg yolk and flute edges of pastry so that a rim forms and crust is attached to casserole. Slash crust in several places to allow steam to escape. Brush top crust with rest of egg yolk. Bake for about 30 minutes at 375° until crust is well browned and filling is bubbly.

GAME PIE

Baking time: approximately 2 hours
Preheat oven to: 450°
Pie pan: deep-dish casserole, 1½ to 2-quart size
Type of crust: puff pastry, single crust
Quantity: six to eight entrée servings
Storing: in refrigerator, covered

1 package frozen puff pastry, for one-crust pie
two 1-lb. Cornish game hens (thawed and quartered)
¾ pound veal cutlet (sliced fairly thick), cut into 1-inch strips
½ pound cooked ham, cut into 1-inch strips
2 tablespoons finely chopped parsley
3 tablespoons finely chopped onion

1 teaspoon seasoned salt
½ teaspoon coarsely ground pepper
6 tablespoons cognac
6 tablespoons red wine
3 tablespoons butter
3 tablespoons olive oil
½ teaspoon sage
¼ pound mushrooms, sliced
1 bay leaf
1 cup strong chicken stock or bouillon
1 egg yolk, beaten, for brushing

This is surely one of the most delicious of meat pies, made with a puff pastry crust.

Marinate chicken, veal, ham, parsley, onion, salt and pepper in combined cognac and red wine overnight. Sauté chicken in combined butter and olive oil until browned. Remove bones and cut meat into bite-size pieces. Mix meats in casserole. Add to marinade the sage, mushrooms, bay leaf and bouillon, and pour over meats in casserole. Dot with butter.

45

Roll out pastry for crust, covering casserole amply. Brush rim of casserole with beaten egg yolk, and flute edges of pastry so that a rim is formed, attaching the crust to the casserole. Slash crust in several places to allow steam to escape. Brush top crust with rest of beaten egg yolk. Bake at 450° for about 20 minutes, reduce temperature to 375° and bake 1½ hours longer, until pastry is golden.

TURKEY-HAM PIE

Baking time: 30-35 minutes
Preheat oven to: 350°
Pie pan: deep-dish casserole, 1½-quart size
Type of crust: pastry, single crust
Quantity: four to six servings
Storing: in refrigerator, covered

½ recipe for two-crust pastry
4 tablespoons butter
¼ cup flour
2 cups strong chicken broth
1 teaspoon seasoned salt
1 teaspoon MSG

½ teaspoon pepper
3 tablespoons chopped parsley
½ cup chopped mushrooms
3 cups cooked chicken, diced
1½ cups cooked ham, diced
¼ cup chopped chives
1 egg, beaten, for brushing

Turkey and ham complement each other in this rich, savory pie.

Blend butter and flour together in a saucepan over a medium heat and add chicken broth, stirring constantly until sauce is thickened. Add all other ingredients (except pastry) and blend well. Pour into casserole.

Prepare, roll out pastry and top casserole. Brush rim of casserole with beaten egg yolk and flute edges of pastry so that a rim is formed and the crust is attached to the casserole. Slash in several places. Brush top with rest of beaten egg yolk. Bake at 350° until crust is browned.

VEAL AND HAM PIE

Baking time: 20 minutes (plus ½ to 1 hour on top of stove)
Preheat oven to: 450°
Pie pan: deep-dish casserole, at least 2-quart size
Type of crust: pastry, single crust
Quantity: eight main dish servings
Storing: in refrigerator, covered

½ recipe for two-crust pastry
1½ pounds veal cut into 1-inch cubes
  (about 3 cups cooked veal)
1½ pounds ham cut into 1-inch cubes
  (about 3 cups cooked ham)
¼ cup flour

4 tablespoons butter
¼ teaspoon salt
¼ teaspoon coarsely ground pepper
1 tablespoon Worcestershire sauce
4 hard-boiled eggs, sliced thickly
a little milk, for brushing

An old English dish, excellent hot or chilled. It can be made with either leftover cooked meat or with fresh.

Coat veal and ham with flour (use more if necessary) and brown in butter. When browned, add enough hot water to cover meats and simmer

47

over low heat (lid on) for about one hour. (If you are using cooked meats, reduce simmering time to 30 minutes.) The sauce should have thickened; if not, sprinkle in flour by the teaspoonful until the sauce is thickened. Remove meat from frying pan to a dish. Add salt, pepper, Worcestershire sauce to pan and stir well to incorporate glaze from bottom of pan.

In a casserole dish, alternate layers of meat with layers of sliced egg. Pour sauce over all. Roll out pastry and top casserole, making sure to extend pastry over the top edge. Slash well. Brush crust with milk and bake casserole about 20 minutes until crust is browned.

ROAST BEEF
OR STEAK PIE

Baking time: 25 minutes
Preheat oven to: 450°
Pie pan: deep-dish casserole, 2-quart size
Type of crust: pastry, single crust
Quantity: six servings
Storing: in refrigerator, covered

---

¹/₂ recipe for two-crust pastry
3¹/₂ cups leftover roast beef or steak (the rarer, the better) cut in 1-inch cubes
3 tablespoons butter
1 large yellow onion, coarsely chopped
2 cloves garlic, mashed
¹/₄ pound mushrooms, sliced
4 tablespoons flour

2¹/₂ cups bouillon
¹/₂ cup port
1 teaspoon MSG
¹/₂ teaspoon salt
¹/₄ teaspoon black pepper, coarsely ground
1 tablespoon Worcestershire sauce
1 tablespoon chopped parsley
1 teaspoon salad herbs
a little milk, for brushing

A marvelously robust pie, the perfect answer to what to do with leftover roast beef or steak.

Pick over roast beef or steak and remove as much fat as possible. Melt butter in frying pan and sauté onion, garlic and mushrooms until lightly browned. Stir in beef and heat through. Remove meat and vegetables from pan, leaving accumulated fat. Stir in flour until smooth, then add all other ingredients (except pastry) and heat thoroughly. Fill casserole with meat and vegetables and pour contents of frying pan over them.

Roll out pastry and top casserole, making sure to extend pastry over edges. Slash well. Brush with milk. Bake at 450° for about 25 minutes until crust is well browned.

STEAK AND KIDNEY PIE

Baking time: about two hours (filling 1½ hours, crust ½ hour)
Preheat oven to: 350°
Pie pan: deep-dish casserole, at least 2-quart size
Type of crust: flaky pastry
Quantity: six to eight servings
Storing: in refrigerator, covered

FILLING

3 pounds round steak (or sliced top of round), cut into 1-inch cubes
½ cup flour
½ cup butter (1 stick)
4 veal kidneys (core and fat removed), sliced
1 cup onions, coarsely chopped
1 pound mushrooms, sliced

½ cup chopped parsley
1 cup beef bouillon
1 cup port wine
½ teaspoon mace
1 tablespoon Worcestershire sauce
1 teaspoon salt
½ teaspoon coarsely ground pepper
1 bay leaf

For optimum results with this old English dish, the filling should be made a day or two beforehand, so the flavors can blend.

PORK PIE

Baking time: 40 minutes
Preheat oven to: 450°
Pie pan: deep-dish casserole, 6-cup
  size
Type of crust: pastry, two-crust
Quantity: six to eight main dish
  servings
Storing: in refrigerator, covered

1 recipe for two-crust pastry
3 cups cold roast pork, cubed in
    1-inch pieces
3 cups cooking apples, pared and
    thickly sliced

½ teaspoon ground cloves
½ teaspoon nutmeg
4 tablespoons sugar
½ cup pork gravy
¼ cup bouillon
a little milk, for brushing

This hearty pie, pungent with tart apples and spices, makes memorable finale to leftover pork roast.

Prepare, roll out half of the pastry and line casserole dish. Alternate layers of pork and apples, sprinkling each apple layer with a dusting of cloves, nutmeg and sugar. Mix gravy and bouillon together and pour over all. Roll out remainder of pastry and top casserole, making sure to extend pastry over edges. Slash well. Brush with milk. Bake for 10 minutes at 450°; lower temperature to 350° and bake for an additional 30 minutes, until crust is browned and apples are cooked through.

LEEK AND SAUSAGE PIE

Baking time: 1½ hours
Preheat oven to: 400°
Pie pan: 9-inch pie pan
Type of crust: pastry, two-crust
Quantity: four to six servings
Storing: lightly covered

---

1 recipe for two-crust pastry
1 lb. leeks (small and young if
    possible)
1 lb. sausage meat, lean

2 eggs
½ teaspoon seasoned salt
¼ teaspoon coarsely ground pepper
1 egg, beaten, for brushing

Very good hot, and even better served cold for luncheon, with a crisp salad.

Prepare pastry, roll out and line pie pan with one half of dough. Wash and trim tough outside leaves from leeks, cut into ½-inch slices. Arrange half of leek slices over rolled out pie dough. Cover with pieces of sausage meat; arrange other half of leek slices over sausage meat. Beat eggs well with salt and pepper and pour over leeks and sausage meat. Roll out remaining pie dough, cover pie, trim edges and crimp. Slash to allow steam to escape. Brush with beaten egg or milk. Bake at 400° for 15 minutes; reduce temperature to 325° and bake for another 1¼ hours until filling is bubbly and the crust golden. If to be served cold, cool on a cooling rack.

Dessert Pies

CUSTARD AND CREAM PIES
CHIFFON PIES
MERINGUE PIES
FRUIT AND BERRY PIES
COBBLERS

CUSTARD PIE

Baking time: 30 minutes
Preheat oven to: 450°
Pie pan: 9-inch pie pan
Type of crust: pastry, single crust
Quantity: six to eight servings
Storing: in refrigerator, covered

1/2 recipe for two-crust pastry
4 eggs, beaten
1/2 cup sugar

1/4 teaspoon salt
1 1/2 teaspoons vanilla
2 1/2 cups scalding milk
nutmeg

Prepare pastry, roll out and line pie pan. Beat together eggs, sugar, salt and vanilla and add scalding milk. Pour into lined pie pan and dust with nutmeg. Put into oven and bake at 450° for 10 minutes, lower oven temperature to 350° and bake another 20 minutes. The center will still be slightly liquid but will solidify during cooling. Cool on a cooling rack. Serve at room temperature or chilled. Garnish with whipped cream.

VARIATIONS
COCONUT CUSTARD PIE
Sprinkle 1 cup of shredded coconut over pie shell before adding custard and sprinkle 1 tablespoon shredded coconut over custard to brown while baking.

ALMOND CUSTARD PIE
Sprinkle 1 cup of browned, slivered almonds over pie shell before adding custard. Add 1 teaspoon almond extract to basic recipe.

CHOCOLATE CUSTARD PIE

Increase sugar to 1 cup and add 2 ounces of melted, unsweetened chocolate to basic recipe. Serve with whipped cream, sprinkled with shaved chocolate.

EGGNOG PIE

Baking time: crust 10 minutes; chilling
time 3 hours
Preheat oven to: 475°
Pie pan: 9-inch pie pan
Type of crust: pastry, single crust
Quantity: six to eight servings
Storing: in refrigerator, lightly covered

one 9-inch baked pie shell, cooled
6 eggs, separated
¼ cup sugar
3 tablespoons dark rum
2 teaspoons vanilla
1½ cups cold light cream

1 tablespoon unflavored gelatin, soaked
in 1 tablespoon cold water
⅓ cup sugar
2 teaspoons nutmeg
whipped cream and shaved chocolate,
for garnish

One of the best of all custard pies.

Beat egg yolks until lemon colored and smooth, add ¼ cup sugar, rum, vanilla and blend well. Then add cream and beat for 3 minutes at medium speed. In a separate bowl, beat egg whites until stiff peaks are formed; fold in egg-yolk mixture and softened gelatin. Pour into cooled, baked pie shell and sprinkle with ⅓ cup sugar mixed with 2 teaspoons nutmeg. Chill for at least three hours before serving. Decorate with whipped cream and shaved chocolate if desired.

HONEYED PUMPKIN PIE

Baking time: 45 minutes
Preheat oven to: 400°
Pie pan: 9-inch baking pan
Type of crust: pastry, single crust
Quantity: six to eight servings
Storing: in refrigerator, covered

½ recipe for two-crust pastry	½ teaspoon allspice
one 16 oz. can pumpkin	1 teaspoon salt
1 teaspoon cinnamon	4 eggs
½ teaspoon nutmeg	1 cup half and half
	1 cup honey

This is lighter in texture than traditional pumpkin pie.

Prepare pastry, line baking pan, fluting edges high. Blend together all other ingredients and beat until completely mixed. Pour into pie shell and bake at 400° for about 30 minutes. Lower temperature to 375° and bake for another 15 minutes, until a knife inserted in middle comes out clean and the top is browned. Cool on a cooling rack. Serve at room temperature with whipped cream.

SOUTHERN PECAN PIE

Baking time: 45 minutes
Preheat oven to: 450°
Pie pan: 9-inch pan
Type of crust: pastry, single crust
Quantity: six to eight servings
Storing: in refrigerator, covered

½ recipe for two-crust pastry
3 eggs
½ teaspoon salt

½ cup dark-brown sugar, well packed
½ cup melted butter (one stick)
1 cup dark corn syrup
1½ cups halved pecans (6 ounces)

Prepare pastry, line baking pan, prick bottom well and bake for about 5 minutes in 450° oven. This high heat may make pastry shrink more than usual, so be sure to allow a generous rim on pie when rolling out. Cool crust on cooling rack; reduce oven temperature to 425°.

Beat together eggs and salt until lemon colored and then continue beating, slowly adding brown sugar. An electric mixer is best for getting the lumps out. Reduce mixer speed to low and drizzle in melted butter and corn syrup. Pour into partly baked pie shell and top with halved pecans. Bake for about ten minutes at 425° and then lower temperature to 325°. Continue baking for another thirty minutes, until crust and top are well browned, and filling is set. Cool on cooling rack. Serve at room temperature.

VANILLA CREAM PIE

Baking time: 10 minutes for pie shell,
15 minutes for meringue (optional)
Preheat oven to: 450°
Pie pan: 9-inch pie pan
Type of crust: pastry, single crust
Quantity: six to eight servings
Storing: in refrigerator, covered

$\frac{1}{2}$ recipe for two-crust pastry
$\frac{1}{2}$ cup cold milk
$\frac{2}{3}$ cup sugar
$\frac{1}{2}$ teaspoon salt
$\frac{1}{4}$ cup cornstarch

3 eggs, separated (if making meringue,
see page 71)
$1\frac{1}{2}$ cups hot milk
1 teaspoon vanilla
2 tablespoons butter

Prepare pastry, roll out and line pie pan. Prick bottom of pastry, flute edges. Bake in a 450° oven for about 10 minutes until evenly browned. Cool.

In a double boiler, combine cold milk, sugar, salt and cornstarch. Beat in egg yolks and gradually add hot milk. Add vanilla and butter. Stir until smooth and thickened. Remove from heat and cool slightly. Pour into baked pie shell. Cover with meringue if using it, and bake for 15 minutes at 350° until browned.

VARIATIONS
CHOCOLATE CREAM PIE
Blend 2 squares of melted unsweetened chocolate into hot milk before

adding to egg mixture. Increase sugar to $3/4$ cup or to taste. Top meringue with shaved chocolate.

CHOCOLATE MINT CREAM PIE
Add 1 teaspoon peppermint extract to above recipe when adding vanilla and butter.

BUTTERSCOTCH CREAM PIE
Substitute $3/4$ cup dark brown sugar for $2/3$ cup white sugar called for in basic recipe. Sprinkle meringue with crushed toffee bars before serving.

COFFEE CREAM PIE
Add 3 tablespoons instant coffee powder to basic recipe. Sprinkle meringue with chopped almonds.

BANANA CREAM PIE
Add three sliced bananas into basic filling before pouring into pie shell.

COCONUT CREAM PIE
Add 1 cut shredded coconut to basic filling before pouring into pie shell. Top meringue before baking with shredded coconut.

Baking time: 20 minutes; chilling time: overnight
Preheat oven to: 375°
Pie pan: two 9-inch pie pans, well greased
Type of crust: slightly chewy, rather like cookie crust
Quantity: two 9-inch pies, each serving twelve people
Storing: in refrigerator, covered

MOCHA CREAM PIE

PIE SHELL
1 package pie crust mix
1/2 cup dark brown sugar
1 1/2 cups ground walnuts (one 8-oz. can shelled walnuts)
2 oz. baking chocolate (2 squares), grated
1 tablespoon vanilla

MOCHA CREAM FILLING
1 cup butter, softened (2 sticks)
1 1/2 cups sugar

1 1/2 tablespoons instant coffee powder
4 eggs
2 oz. baking chocolate (2 squares), melted and cooled

TOPPING
4 cups heavy cream (one quart)
4 tablespoons instant coffee powder
1 cup confectioners sugar
1 1/2 cups sliced almonds (two 6 oz. packages)
2 oz. baking chocolate (2 squares), grated coarsely or shaved

This is one of the richest and prettiest pies imaginable.

Make crust by combining all *Pie Shell* ingredients (if using buttercrust mix, follow package directions — adding butter and water — before com-

63

bining with other ingredients in this recipe) and mix with a fork to blend well. Divide mixture in half and turn each half into a greased 9-inch pie plate. With the back of a tablespoon, mold the dough to fit the pie pan, dipping spoon into hot water to prevent dough from sticking to spoon. This dough shrinks more than most doughs, so be sure to form a wide, full edge on the pies. Prick bottoms with a fork and bake about 20 minutes. Cool pie pans on a cooling rack.

Make mocha filling by combining all *Mocha Cream Filling* ingredients, and beat with an electric mixer at low speed for 10 minutes. Turn into completely cooled pie shells, cover and refrigerate overnight before topping is added.

Several hours before serving, combine in a large bowl the heavy cream, instant coffee and sugar, as listed in *Topping* ingredients, and refrigerate for about an hour, stirring occasionally so that the sugar and instant coffee dissolve completely. About an hour before serving, whip coffee-cream mixture until stiff. Spread thickly over pie with a broad knife, completely covering filling and crust. Sprinkle with sliced almonds and shaved chocolate, and refrigerate pie until serving.

Note that shell and filling can be made in advance and kept (separately) in the freezer, to be defrosted and combined later, and topped before serving.

LEMON OR LIME CHIFFON PIE

Baking time: 10 minutes for pie shell
Preheat oven to: 450°
Pie pan: 9-inch pie pan
Type of crust: graham cracker crumb
    or gingersnap crust
Quantity: six to eight servings
Storing: in refrigerator, lightly covered

1 recipe for graham cracker crumb
    crust or gingersnap crust (see
    page 17)
1 envelope unflavored gelatin, softened
    in 1 tablespoon water

4 eggs, separated
1 cup sugar
$3/4$ cup lemon or lime juice
finely grated rind of two limes or
    lemons
sugar

This is an airy, light pie with plenty of flavor. If too tart for your taste, more sugar can be added to the egg whites.

Prepare crust and bake for about 10 minutes until lightly browned and cohesive. Cool.

In the top of a double boiler, combine softened gelatin, egg yolks, $1/2$ cup sugar and juice. Heat, stirring constantly until thickened. Add rind and remove from heat. If you are making lime chiffon pie, you may want to add a few drops of blue food coloring to the mixture to make it greener.

Beat egg whites until foamy and slowly beat in $1/2$ cup sugar (or more, to taste). Fold cooled lime mixture into egg whites and pour into pie shell. Sprinkle with grated rind mixed with double its amount of sugar. Chill pie for at least two hours before serving.

VARIATION
CITRUS CHIFFON PIE
Instead of lemon or lime juice alone, use the juices of 2 medium lemons, 1 medium orange and $1/2$ medium grapefruit and the combined rinds of 1 lemon, 1 orange and $1/2$ a grapefruit.

FRUIT CHIFFON PIE
(Strawberry, Raspberry, Apple, Pineapple, Apricot, Cherry)

Baking time: 10 minutes, pie shell
Preheat oven to: 450°
Pie pan: 9-inch pie pan
Type of crust: pastry, single crust
Quantity: six to eight servings
Storing: in refrigerator, covered

½ recipe for two-crust pastry
¾ cup apple juice
1 cup sugar (or more, to taste)
1 envelope unflavored gelatin, softened in 1 tablespoon water
4 eggs, separated
2 tablespoons lemon juice

1 cup pureed fresh fruit (or dried apricots soaked in water for 1 hour, cooked and drained)
½ teaspoon cream of tartar
¼ teaspoon salt
½ teaspoon almond extract (for cherry or apricot only)
whipped cream for garnish

Prepare pastry, roll out, line pie pan. Prick bottom and flute edges. Bake for about 10 minutes until evenly browned. Cool.

In a saucepan, combine apple juice, ½ cup sugar, softened gelatin, egg yolks and lemon juice. Stir constantly over medium heat until thickened. Stir in fruit puree and cool.

Beat egg whites with cream of tartar and salt until foamy. Slowly beat in ½ cup sugar until stiff and glossy. Fold in fruit mixture and pour into cooled, baked pie shell. Refrigerate at least two hours until set. Garnish with whipped cream and whole pieces of the fruit used.

VARIATION
CRANBERRY CHIFFON PIE
Use 1 cup of whole cranberry sauce instead of fruit puree.

CHOCOLATE CHIFFON PIE

Baking time: 10 minutes for crust
Preheat oven to: 450°
Pie pan: 9-inch pie pan
Type of crust: pastry, single crust, or
    chocolate wafer crumb
Quantity: six to eight servings
Storing: in refrigerator, covered

½ recipe for two-crust pastry or 1
    recipe for crumb crust
1 cup sugar
2 ounces unsweetened chocolate,
    melted
½ cup strong coffee

4 eggs, separated
1 envelope unflavored gelatin softened
    in ¼ cup cold water
½ teaspoon vanilla
whipped cream and shaved chocolate
    for garnish

Prepare pie crust, line pie pan, flute edges. Bake until lightly browned and set. Cool.

In a double boiler, combine ½ cup of sugar, melted chocolate, coffee and egg yolks. Stir until blended and add softened gelatin. Continue stirring over simmering water until thickened.

Beat egg whites until frothy and gradually add remaining sugar, a little at a time. Continue beating until glossy and stiff. Fold chocolate mixture into egg whites and pour into baked, cooled pie shell. Refrigerate at least two hours and decorate with whipped cream, chopped nuts or chocolate jimmies.

LEMON MERINGUE PIE

Baking time: 25 minutes (crust 10 minutes, meringue 15 minutes)
Preheat oven to: 450°
Pie pan: 9-inch pie pan
Type of crust: pastry, single crust
Quantity: six to eight servings

1/2 recipe for two-crust pastry
1/2 cup cornstarch
1 1/2 cups sugar
1/2 teaspoon salt
1 1/2 cups boiling water
3 eggs, separated

2 tablespoons butter
1 tablespoon grated lemon rind
3/4 cup fresh lemon juice
1/4 teaspoon cream of tartar
1/4 teaspoon salt
1/2 teaspoon vanilla
1/4 cup sugar

Prepare pastry, roll out and line pie pan. Flute edges, prick bottom. Bake until evenly browned for about 10 minutes in a 450° oven. Cool and reduce temperature to 350°.

In a saucepan, combine cornstarch, sugar, salt and boiling water. Stir over medium heat until smooth. Boil for one minute. Turn off heat and add egg yolks, butter, lemon rind and lemon juice. Stir quickly until thickened. You may need to turn on heat again to thicken properly but do not allow to boil. When thick, pour into cooled pie shell.

To make meringue, beat egg whites with cream of tartar, salt and vanilla until glossy. Slowly add 1/4 cup sugar and continue beating until stiff. Spread with a knife evenly over lemon filling and bake pie at 350°

69

for about 15 minutes, until meringue is browned. Cool on cooling rack and chill before serving.

VARIATION
BLACK BOTTOM LEMON PIE
Melt 3 ounces (3 squares) of semisweet chocolate and spread over cooled pie shell before adding lemon filling.

KEY LIME PIE

Baking time: 25 minutes (crust 10 minutes, meringue 15 minutes)
Preheat oven to: 450°
Pie pan: 9-inch pie pan
Type of crust: pastry, single crust
Quantity: six to eight servings

½ recipe for two-crust pastry
⅓ cup cornstarch
1½ cups sugar
¼ teaspoon salt
1¼ cups water
½ cup fresh lime juice

1 tablespoon finely grated lime peel
3 eggs, separated
green food coloring
¼ teaspoon cream of tartar
¼ teaspoon salt
½ teaspoon vanilla
¼ cup sugar

Prepare pastry and line pie pan, flute edges. Bake at 450° for about 10 minutes until evenly browned. Cool. Reduce oven temperature to 350°.

In a saucepan, combine cornstarch, sugar, salt and water. Boil for one minute, stirring constantly. Turn off heat and add lime juice, peel and egg yolks, stirring quickly until thickened. You may need to turn on heat again to thicken properly. Add food coloring for a more attractive color. When thick, pour into cooled pie shell.

To make meringue follow directions given on p. 69. Cool on cooling rack and chill before serving.

MANDARIN ORANGE MERINGUE

Baking time: 25 minutes (crust 10 minutes, meringue 15)
Preheat oven to: 450°
Pie pan: 9-inch pie pan
Type of crust: pastry, single crust
Quantity: six to eight servings

½ recipe for two-crust pastry
4 eggs, separated
¼ cup frozen orange juice concentrate
1 tablespoon lemon juice
2 tablespoons water
1 tablespoon fresh grated orange peel

¼ cup sugar
2 cans mandarin oranges, drained
¼ teaspoon cream of tartar
¼ teaspoon salt
½ teaspoon vanilla
¼ cup sugar

Prepare pastry, roll out and line pie pan. Prick bottom, flute edges. Bake until evenly browned, about 10 minutes in a 450° oven. Cool.

In a double boiler combine egg yolks, juice concentrate, lemon juice, water, orange peel and sugar. Heat over bubbling water, stirring constantly until thickened. Remove from heat and fold in drained oranges. Pour into cooled pie shell.

Prepare meringue as on p. 69. Cool. Serve chilled.

PEACH MERINGUE PIE

Baking time: one hour
Preheat oven to: 400°
Pie pan: 9-inch pie pan
Type of crust: pastry, no top crust
Quantity: six to eight servings

$^1/_2$ recipe for two-crust pastry
4 packages (12 oz. each) frozen
    peaches, a scant 4 cups drained
juice $^1/_2$ lemon
1 teaspoon almond extract

3 tablespoons quick-cooking tapioca
1 tablespoon butter
3 egg whites
$^1/_4$ teaspoon salt
6 tablespoons sugar

Roll out pastry and line pie pan, fluting edges high. Combine peaches, lemon juice, almond extract and tapioca in a bowl; stir well to coat peaches and let stand $^1/_2$ hour. When tapioca has softened ($^1/_2$ hour), turn peaches into lined pie pan, dot with butter and cover peaches (not pastry) with a double thickness of aluminum foil — this will keep the peaches from browning. Bake for about 50 minutes, or until the crust is browned. Remove from oven and discard foil.

In a medium bowl, combine egg whites and salt and beat until soft peaks form. Add sugar, a tablespoonful at a time, until meringue is stiff. With a broad knife, swirl meringue on top of peaches, sealing the edges of peaches and crust. Bake in the oven for another 5 to 10 minutes (watch carefully) until nicely browned. Cool on a cooling rack.

ALTERNATE METHOD WITH FRESH PEACHES
Use a scant four cups of fresh, sliced peaches (six to eight peaches of

good size) to which you add $^3/_4$ cup of sugar before combining with tapioca, lemon juice and extract.

CITRUS ANGEL PIE
(Orange, Lemon, Lime or Grapefruit)

Baking time: 1 hour
Preheat oven to: 275°
Pie pan: 9-inch pie pan, buttered
Type of crust: meringue
Quantity: six to eight servings

MERINGUE CRUST (see recipe p. 18)

FILLING
$^1/_4$ cup frozen orange or grapefruit
    juice concentrate, fresh lemon or
    lime juice
$1^1/_2$ tablespoons grated fresh rind of
    citrus you're using

4 egg yolks
$^1/_2$ cup sugar
1 cup heavy cream, whipped

GARNISHES (optional)
toasted slivered almonds
grated fresh rind mixed with twice its
    quantity of sugar
grated bitter chocolate

Angel pies are baked in a meringue pie shell rather than a pastry or crumb shell.

Make meringue crust as directed.
  To make filling, in a double boiler, beat together concentrate or juice,

74

rind, egg yolks and sugar and cook until thickened over gently bubbling water. Cool. Whip cream until stiff. Fold one half whipped cream into egg yolk mixture until completely blended. Spread half of remaining whipped cream over meringue shell. Fill shell with citrus filling and cover with remainder of whipped cream. Chill several hours before serving. Garnish as desired.

OLD-FASHIONED APPLE PIE

Baking time: 45-50 minutes
Preheat oven to: 450°
Pie pan: 9-inch pie pan
Type of crust: pastry, double crust
Quantity: six to eight servings
Storing: at room temperature, loosely covered

1 recipe for two-crust pastry
8 McIntosh apples, peeled, cored and sliced in eighths
1 cup dark brown sugar
juice and grated rind 1 lemon

½ teaspoon nutmeg
2 teaspoons cinnamon
2 tablespoons butter
1 egg, beaten, or a little milk, for brushing

This pie is tart, sweet and rich with brown sugar and cinnamon. Best served warm.

Prepare pastry, roll out and line pie pan with one half. Arrange sliced apples in layers and sprinkle each layer with mixture of brown sugar, lemon rind and juice, nutmeg and cinnamon. Dot top of pie with butter and cover with top crust. Flute edges and slash well. Brush top crust with milk or beaten egg and bake at 450° for 15 minutes. Lower temperature to 350° and continue baking for another 30 minutes, or until top crust is well browned. Cool to warm or room temperature.

VARIATIONS

DEEP-DISH APPLE PIE

Fill a 1½-quart casserole with apples and top with ½ pastry. Slash and bake as with two-crust pie.

APPLE RAISIN PIE

Add ½ cup of raisins to basic filling.

ENGLISH APPLE PIE

Add two egg yolks and 1 cup of heavy cream to basic filling recipe before baking. This filling has a slightly custardy texture and is quite rich.

FRESH FRUIT PIE
(Peach, Nectarine, Pear or Plum)

Type of pie: dessert
Baking time: 35-40 minutes
Preheat oven to: 425°
Pie pan: 9-inch pie pan
Type of crust: pastry, lattice crust
Quantity: six to eight servings
Storing: in refrigerator, lightly covered

1 recipe for two-crust pastry
5 cups fresh sliced firm, ripe fruit,
    cored and pared
juice and grated rind of 1 lemon
1 cup sugar (adjust according to
    ripeness and sweetness of fruit)

1 teaspoon cinnamon
$1/2$ teaspoon nutmeg
2 tablespoons quick-cooking tapioca
2 tablespoons butter ($1/4$ stick)
1 egg, beaten, or a little milk, for
    brushing

For variety, try any combination of these fruits.

Prepare pastry, roll out and line pie pan with one half of dough.

In a mixing bowl, combine fruit, lemon rind, juice, sugar, cinnamon, nutmeg and tapioca. Stir to blend and turn into pie shell. Dot with butter. Roll out remaining pastry, cut strips for lattice top and weave crust crimping edges. Brush with milk or beaten egg. Bake at 425° for about 15 minutes; reduce temperature to 350° and bake for another 25 minutes until crust is golden and the filling bubbly. Cool to warm or room temperature.

VARIATIONS
DEEP DISH PIE
Fill 1½-quart casserole with fruit filling and top with ½ recipe for crust. Slash to allow steam to escape, brush with beaten egg or milk and bake as above.

FRUIT PIE WITH CHEESE
Cheddar cheese adds a marvelous flavor to most fruit pies. Add ½ cup grated sharp cheddar, sprinkled over top of filling when dotting with butter before putting crust on.

ALTERNATE METHODS WITH CANNED OR FROZEN FRUIT
PEACHES AND NECTARINES
Canned, use two 1-pound cans of freestone peaches, or nectarines, sliced and well drained. You will probably need only ⅓ cup of sugar (if that) with either canned or frozen peaches. Use three 11-ounce packages of frozen peaches, thawed and well drained.

PEARS AND PLUMS
Use two 1-pound cans of either fruit (be sure to take pits out of plums), drain well. You will probably not need more than ⅓ cup of sugar.

FRESH CHERRY PIE

Baking time: 40 minutes
Preheat oven to: 425°
Pie pan: 9-inch pie pan
Type of crust: pastry, lattice crust
Quantity: six to eight servings
Storing: in refrigerator, covered

---

1 recipe for two-crust pastry
4½ cups fresh, tart cherries, washed and pitted
1 cup sugar (adjust according to sweetness of fruit)
grated rind of 1 lemon

1 teaspoon almond extract
¼ cup cornstarch
¼ teaspoon salt
2 tablespoons butter (¼ stick)
1 egg, beaten, or a little milk, for brushing

When cherries are plentiful and ripe, this is a crowning glory to any meal. For variety, use equal amounts of tart red cherries and sweeter, darker cherries.

Combine cherries, sugar, lemon rind, extract, cornstarch and salt. Mix well and let stand while making pie crust.

Prepare pie crust, roll out and line 9-inch pie pan with one half dough. Pour in cherry filling. Dot with butter. Roll out top crust and weave a lattice top, crimping and fluting edges. Brush with milk or beaten egg. Bake for about 40 minutes (watch after 30 minutes for over browning of crust — cover with aluminum foil if necessary). Crust should be well browned and filling bubbly. Cool on a cooling rack.

VARIATION
CHERRY PIE WITH CANNED FRUIT

two 1-pound cans water pack cherries
3 tablespoons quick-cooking tapioca
½ teaspoon salt
1 teaspoon almond extract
juice and grated rind of 1 lemon

1½ cups sugar
red food coloring
2 tablespoons butter for dotting before
   baking
1 recipe for two-crust pastry

Combine the first seven ingredients and let stand while preparing pastry. Proceed as with fresh cherry pie.

FRESH BERRY PIE
(Blackberry, Blueberry, Elderberry, Gooseberry, Loganberry)

Baking time: approximately 45 minutes
Preheat oven to: 450°
Pie pan: 9-inch pie pan
Type of crust: pastry, lattice crust
Quantity: six to eight servings
Storing: in refrigerator, covered

---

1 recipe for two-crust pastry
4 cups fresh berries, washed and picked over
1 cup sugar (to be adjusted according to ripeness and sweetness of fruit)
2 tablespoons quick-cooking tapioca

juice and grated rind of ½ lemon (increase to 1 lemon if fruit is very bland)
¼ teaspoon salt
2 tablespoons butter (¼ stick)
1 egg, beaten, or a little milk for brushing

Combine fruit, sugar, tapioca, lemon juice and rind, and salt and set aside while making pastry.

Prepare pastry, roll out and line pie pan with one half. Pour in fruit filling, dot with butter. Roll out top crust, cut into strips and weave a lattice top, crimping and fluting edges. Brush with milk or beaten egg and bake at 450° for 10 minutes. Reduce temperature to 350° and bake for 35 minutes longer until crust is browned and berries are tender. Cool on a cooling rack.

VARIATIONS
Deep-dish pies can be made from this recipe by using a casserole (1- to 1½-quart size) for filling and using half the recipe for crust. Slash crust and bake as above.

SPICY BERRY PIE
Substitute brown sugar for white in basic recipe and add 1 teaspoon ground cloves and 1 teaspoon cinnamon to basic filling.

ALTERNATE METHOD WITH CANNED OR FROZEN BERRIES
Canned or frozen berries can be substituted for fresh fruit (be sure to drain well), but their flavor and texture is not as pleasing as that of fresh fruit.

FRESH STRAWBERRY PIE

Baking time: 45 minutes
Preheat oven to: 450°
Pie pan: 9-inch pie pan
Type of crust: pastry, lattice crust
Quantity: six to eight servings

1 recipe for two-crust pastry
3½ cups fresh, ripe, whole strawberries (about two pint baskets, picked over, stems and blemishes cut out. You may need more if fruit is not fully ripe or is bruised.)

3 tablespoons cornstarch
½ cup sugar
¼ teaspoon salt
1 tablespoon butter
1 egg, beaten, for brushing

Because strawberries are such a fragile fruit, this pie does not keep well and is best served the day it is made. A dollop of sweetened sour cream on top is a fine addition.

Roll out pastry for bottom crust, line pie pan. Combine strawberries, cornstarch, sugar and salt. Gently fold together to coat strawberries completely; turn into pastry-lined pan. Roll out remaining pastry and cut into strips. Dot strawberries with butter and cover with woven lattice top. Brush top crust with beaten egg. Bake pie at 450° for ten minutes; reduce temperature to 350° and bake for another 35 minutes until crust is browned and the filling is bubbly. This is a very juicy pie, so take care in handling. Cool on a rack before refrigerating. Serve cold.

ALTERNATE METHOD WITH FROZEN STRAWBERRIES

Use only whole berries; one 16 oz. cup yields about 1 cup of fruit and 1 cup of juice. Thaw and drain four 16 oz. cups and follow directions as above, but add only ¼ cup of sugar and increase cornstarch to 3½ tablespoons. You may find that the color of the filling is a bit pallid when you use frozen berries and a few drops of red food coloring are needed.

RHUBARB OR PINEAPPLE PIE

Baking time: 45 minutes
Preheat oven to: 425°
Pie pan: 9-inch pie pan
Type of crust: pastry, lattice crust
Quantity: six to eight servings
Storing: in refrigerator, covered

1 recipe for two-crust pastry
4 cups fresh rhubarb, cut in 1-inch pieces or 3 cups shredded fresh pineapple
1¹/₃ cups sugar (adjust according to freshness and sweetness of fruit)
¹/₃ cup cornstarch

1 teaspoon grated orange or lemon peel
juice ¹/₂ lemon (for pineapple only)
2 tablespoons butter (¹/₄ stick)
red food coloring (for rhubarb only, if it needs it)
1 egg, beaten, or a little milk, for brushing

Combine all ingredients for filling and stir once. Set aside.

Prepare pastry, roll out and line pie pan with one half. Pour in filling and dot with butter. Roll out top crust, cut lattice strips. Weave lattice top, crimping edges. Brush with beaten egg or milk and bake at 425° for about 45 minutes until crust is browned and fruit is tender. Cool on a cooling rack.

VARIATIONS
STRAWBERRY-RHUBARB PIE
Substitute 2 cups of fresh, hulled strawberries for 2 cups of the rhubarb.

STRAWBERRY-RHUBARB-PINEAPPLE PIE
Use equal amounts of strawberries, rhubarb and fresh pineapple.

THREE GRAPE PIE

Baking time: 45 minutes
Preheat oven to: 425°
Pie pan: 10-inch pie pan
Type of crust: pastry, no top crust
Quantity: eight to ten servings
Storing: in refrigerator, lightly covered

1 recipe for two-crust pastry
3 cups seeded, halved white grapes
    about 1½ lbs.)
3 cups seeded, halved red (Tokay)
    grapes (about 1½ lbs.)
3 cups seeded, halved black (Ribier)
    grapes (about 1½ lbs.)

1½ cups sugar
4 tablespoons lemon juice
1½ tablespoons grated orange peel,
    fresh
3 tablespoons quick-cooking tapioca
a little milk, for brushing

This pie is a beauty. Each variety of grape is turned into the pie shell separately, in rows or circles, so the colors are distinct.

Using a small bowl for each variety of grape, combine grapes, ½ cup sugar, 1⅓ tablespoons lemon juice, ½ tablespoon orange peel, and 1 tablespoon tapioca in each of the bowls. Stir well to coat grapes evenly. Let stand for 30 minutes.

Roll out pastry and line 10-inch pie pan. Trim and flute pastry fairly high. Turn each of grape mixtures into the pie pan separately, either circling one around the next, or in strips, keeping the colors separate. Brush edge of crust with milk. Bake at 425° about 45 minutes until the grapes are bubbly and the crust is browned. Cool on a cooling rack and serve at room temperature.

CRANBERRY RAISIN PIE

Baking time: 50 minutes
Preheat oven to: 425°
Pie pan: 9-inch pie pan
Type of crust: pastry, lattice crust
Quantity: six to eight servings
Storing: at room temperature, lightly covered

1 recipe for two-crust pastry
3½ cups fresh cranberries (one 12 oz. box, well picked over), washed
2½ tablespoons flour
2 cups sugar
½ teaspoon salt

⅔ cup boiling water
1 tablespoon grated fresh lemon peel
1 cup seedless raisins (8 oz., well packed)
1 tablespoon vanilla
1½ tablespoons butter
a little milk, for brushing

This is a tart-sweet pie, very good with vanilla ice cream or hard sauce.

Roll out pastry for bottom crust, line pie shell. In a saucepan, combine cranberries, flour, sugar, salt, boiling water, lemon peel and raisins. Cover and cook over a medium flame until cranberries begin to pop out of their jackets. Uncover and stir well. Set aside to cool uncovered until lukewarm. Stir in vanilla and butter and turn into pastry-lined pan.

Roll out lattice strips and weave top crust, trimming and fluting edges. Brush top crust with milk and bake at 425° for about 50 minutes, until filling bubbles and crust is browned. Cool on a cooling rack, and serve warm. Reheat, if necessary, in oven before serving.

TWO RAISIN PIE

Baking time: 40 to 45 minutes
Preheat oven to: 425°
Pie pan: 9-inch pie pan
Type of crust: pastry, lattice crust
Quantity: six to eight servings
Storing: lightly covered, at room
temperature

---

1 recipe for two-crust pastry
1 cup orange juice, preferably fresh
3 tablespoons lemon juice
1/2 cup honey
1/4 teaspoon salt
fine grated rind of one orange

3 tablespoons cornstarch
sugar (optional, to taste)
1 tablespoon vanilla
2 1/4 cups well-packed, seedless white
and dark raisins (about 16 oz.)
1 tablespoon butter
a little milk, for brushing

In a saucepan, combine orange juice, lemon juice, honey, cold water, salt and grated orange rind. Boil for one minute. Add cornstarch a little at a time and stir constantly over a medium flame until thickened. Add sugar if necessary. Remove from heat and add vanilla, raisins and butter. Stir well and set aside, so that the raisins will plump up.

Prepare pastry. Roll out bottom crust and line pie pan. Fill with raisin filling, top with lattice or full top crust. Trim excess pastry, flute edges and brush top crust with milk. Bake about 45 minutes, until the filling is bubbly and the top crust is browned. Cool on a cooling rack and serve warm. If necessary, reheat in oven.

HOMEMADE MINCEMEAT PIE

Baking time: approximately 45 minutes
Preheat oven to: 425°
Pie pan: 9-inch pie pan
Type of crust: pastry, lattice crust
Quantity: six generous servings
Storing: lightly covered

1 recipe for two-crust pastry
½ pound lean beef, cut for stewing
scant ¼ lb. ground beef suet
2 cooking apples, Greenings preferred,
    peeled, cored and quartered
2 tablespoons molasses
½ cup cider, fresh or reconstituted
    frozen, if possible
¾ cup dark brown sugar
½ lb. currants
½ lb. mixed white and dark raisins
2 tablespoons diced candied citron

2 tablespoons diced dried apricots
juice and grated rind ½ lemon
½ teaspoon cinnamon
½ teaspoon allspice
¼ teaspoon nutmeg
¼ teaspoon mace
¼ teaspoon ground cloves
¼ cup chopped walnuts
¼ cup sweet sherry or dark rum
¼ cup whiskey or brandy
1 egg beaten, or a little milk, for
    brushing

The classic pie for holidays. Always at its best served warm, accompanied by hard sauce, brandy butter or vanilla ice cream.

In enough water to half cover, boil beef until soft (1 to 2 hours, or more). Lift out the meat, shred it and return to the cook pot. Add suet, apples, molasses, cider, and sugar. Cook briskly until it comes to the boil, add remaining fruits and lemon juice and rind. Reduce fire and simmer, stir-

90

ring constantly, until the mincemeat is thickened. Add spices and continue simmering until liquid has been reduced and mixture is very thick. Stir in walnuts and spirits. Set aside to cool.

Prepare pastry and roll out bottom crust. Line pie pan and fill with mincemeat. You will probably have more mincemeat than you need. Roll out top crust, cut into strips and weave into a lattice top crust, crimping edges. Brush with milk or beaten egg. Bake at about 425° until golden brown. If edges appear to be browning too quickly, cover with aluminum foil, removing foil for the final 15 minutes of baking.

VARIATIONS

Commercially made mincemeat, packed either in glass jars or in a dry form needing addition of water (try adding cider instead) are very good. The addition of 1/4 cup of dark rum and 1/4 cup of brandy will make them even better. You will need about 4 cups of mincemeat for a 9-inch pie.

APRICOT PRUNE PIE

Baking time: 30 minutes
Preheat oven to: 400°
Pie pan: 9-inch pie pan
Type of crust: pastry, lattice crust
Quantity: six to eight servings
Storing: lightly covered at room temperature; for best flavor, serve warm

---

1 recipe for two-crust pastry
1 cup dried prunes, pitted, halved, rinsed and drained (6 oz.)
1 cup dried apricots, rinsed and drained (6 oz.)
½ cup dried currants or chopped raisins (3 oz.)

½ cup dark brown sugar
juice and rind ½ lemon
½ teaspoon salt
1 teaspoon cinnamon
½ teaspoon nutmeg
1 egg, beaten, or a little milk, for brushing

A good breakfast pie, served warm with bacon or sausages.

In a medium saucepan, cover prunes with boiling water and cook for 15 minutes. Drain and reserve ¾ cup of liquid. Combine apricots (uncooked), prunes, currants, prune liquid, sugar, lemon rind and juice, salt, cinnamon and nutmeg in saucepan and simmer about five minutes until thickened. Cool while preparing pastry.

Prepare, roll out pastry and line pie pan with one half. Roll out other half and make lattice strips. Fill unbaked pie shell with prune-apricot filling, and weave lattice top, trimming and fluting edges. Brush top with beaten egg or milk. Bake at 400° for about 30 minutes until crust is well browned and filling bubbly. Cool to warm or room temperature on cooling rack.

FRESH FRUIT COBBLER
(Peach, Cherry, Plum, Pear, Apple, Blueberry, Blackberry)

Baking time: about 1 hour
Preheat oven to: 350°
Pie pan: 10" x 6" x 2" casserole, greased
Type of crust: biscuit
Quantity: eight servings
Storing: in refrigerator

Cobbler biscuit dough (if hurried, packaged biscuit mix will do, prepare as package directs)
2 cups flour
4 teaspoons baking powder
1/2 teaspoon salt
2 tablespoons sugar
1/2 cup shortening
3/4 cup milk

Fruit Filling
3 cups sliced, pitted, peeled fruit
2 tablespoons lemon juice
1/2 to 1 cup sugar (depending on sweetness of fruit)
grated rind of lemon or orange
1 1/2 tablespoons cornstarch
1 cup boiling water
1 teaspoon nutmeg
1/2 teaspoon cinnamon

Cobblers are deep-dish, crustless pies with a biscuit-dough topping dropped on unevenly, giving a cobbled effect. All cobblers should be served warm, with ice cream, whipped cream, sweet or sour cream.

Prepare biscuit dough by working all dry ingredients together, cut in shortening, then add milk. Toss mixture just until it holds together. If using packaged mix, prepare as directed.

Arrange fruit over bottom of greased baking dish. Combine all other filling ingredients in a saucepan and boil for one minute until thickened. Pour over fruit. Drop biscuit dough unevenly to give a cobbled effect over top of fruit. Do not smooth out. Bake at 350° for about an hour until biscuits are cooked and browned and the filling is bubbly. Cool to warm or room temperature before serving.

VARIATION USING CANNED FRUIT
The flavor of canned fruits is not as memorable as that of fresh fruits, but if you don't have the time to prepare fresh fruit, use $2\frac{1}{2}$ cups of canned fruit (a 1-lb. 13 oz. can). Omit water from recipe and reduce sugar to $\frac{1}{4}$ to $\frac{1}{2}$ cup. Frozen peaches, drained and thawed, may be used for Peach Cobbler; proceed as with fresh fruit.

Any of the above fruits in combination make fine cobblers.

NEW ENGLAND COBBLER

Baking time: 50 minutes
Preheat oven to: 400°
Pie pan: shallow 8-cup baking dish, buttered
Type of crust: biscuit
Quantity: eight servings
Storing: in refrigerator, covered; serve warm

---

2 cups dry biscuit mix
6 medium cooking apples, McIntosh preferred
1 cup sugar
1/2 cup dark brown sugar
1/3 cup flour
1 teaspoon ground nutmeg
1/2 teaspoon cinnamon
2 cups cranberry juice
2/3 cups milk
2 teaspoons grated fresh lemon rind

Core, pare and cut apples into eighths. Fill baking dish with apples. Mix together 3/4 cup sugar, brown sugar, flour, nutmeg and cinnamon until well blended. Add cranberry juice and stir until mixture is smooth; pour evenly over apples. Cover baking dish with aluminum foil and bake at 400° for about thirty minutes — the apples should be tender.

In a small bowl, combine 2 tablespoons sugar, milk and biscuit mix. Remove aluminum foil from apples and drop biscuit mix dough by tablespoonfuls over apples. Do not smooth dough out, it should have a cobbled look, with bits of apple showing through. Mix together remaining 2 tablespoons of sugar with grated lemon rind and sprinkle over biscuit dough. Bake until biscuits are browned, about twenty minutes. Cool on a cooling rack to serving temperature. If necessary, warm in oven before serving.